She breathes between the lines

Thingamphy Horam

First Published in October 2021

ISBN: 978-93-5472-856-3

BLUEROSE PUBLISHERS

www.bluerosepublishers.com

info@bluerosepublishers.com

+91 8882 898 898

Cover Design:

Muskan Sachdeva

Typographic Design:

Ilma Miza

Distributed by: BlueRose, Amazon, Flipkart

Dedicated

To my parents who always support me with love and compassion

Preface

This book offers a collection of short verses and lines that I penned for the sheer pleasure of writing them. Words inspire me to write because they act as a catalyst for my amateur imagination. Words are too heavy a burden to carry and the only way I could set myself free from this bondage was to express all of my suppressed thoughts through lines. To all the people who carry their un- spoken thoughts, feelings and emo- tions, I devote this book to you!

This book is a reflection of where I have been in my life as well as my relationships with the individuals I have met and grown up with, the people I have loved, and the people I am bound to meet in the future. Nothing with- out the narrow and curvy odyssey I travel.

Acknowledgement

Thankful to everyone who nudged my memories and who contributed to my astonishing life. Without you, I wouldn't be able to formed and painted my feelings and emotion into words

Content

Marigold Heart 2
Essences 30
Possessed 56
My Sunshine 73
Sprouting with Season 104
Watering 132
Budding 156
Bouquet of daffodils 181

Every last day of relationship break into pieces

Marigold Heart

Intuition

My intuition tells me that I have fallen in the arm of an incurable pain

Are you the pain my intuition tells me to endure?

We stay

We both know

we are no good for each other

But we stayed without regrets

Bitter sweet

You taught me how to be brave and wrecked me at the same time

Exhausted

The day our eyes stop searching for miracles

May be our soul too was too tired to hold everything together

Wave

Those uncountable sorry and

Repeated good-byes

If this is how you make wave out of "I love you"

Don't say at all because love has lost it's meaning

Perception

I used to think of you as someone who will never hurt me

But I was wrong

Different shades

Lilac sky dies in my mind

But you thought of sun

Yellow wasn't for me

Just like lilac was not yours

Space

The distance between sky and earth is closer than the space between us

We weren't

Sorry we couldn't be good at words because we blame each other and fail to rectify and confess that went wrong between us

Too much

You showed me too much of you to lose you

He

He drew the line to paint my own silver lining

Dear you

Dear mama

I am as beautiful as the rest of all girls

I was raised by a wonderful mother

I am not a monster, kindness resides in me

And I have a heart full of love

Mama, all beautiful things does have boundaries

Though we share the same landscape

Dear Papa

I revere you for being a good husband and an understanding father

I hope you understand how it feels like to be a woman

And how to treat her delicately

My papa taught me how to love

To be a woman of strength

He taught me how forgiveness triumph in the end

He is the reason I can accept the rejection thought its humiliating

Dear you!

Where were you?

What were you doing?

All this years

How much of you have taught me how a man should treat a woman

And I realize you are the book I left with a bookmark on the shelf

But when you left

I realize how strong I am

Wasted photograph

He used to keep my photograph in his wallet's pocket when we were together

Now, I wander how many photographs has his warm unseasoned wallet comforted

Or got me thinking, is it just a guy thing to flood their wallet's pocket with girls photograph to validate his manliness

Like everyone else

The sunset shimmer slowly on the warm roof and a golden ray rested on my hair like a crown.

The gust of wind gently ripples on my

face

She carried the purest air

I took the deepest breath, as if I was breathing my last

But now she's gone like everyone else...

Was she only meant to be in the background of my life

Just like I was in hers?

Then I saw the dark cloud covering

The face of the sun and as the darkness approaches

She swiftly disappear like everyone else

Before I could even whisper my farewell.

Back to stranger

He hesitantly said

The woman...The woman

I loved unconditionally..

She Changed

Then, we changed in reverse

Back to strangers

Will the memories bring them back together???

Are they meant to be strangers with memories???

Roadless

In his restless lair, he sighed with a seared voice.

He hid his pounding heart in his words,

Many of his thoughts swamped in memories

His countless lonesome night didn't die down, still haunts him.

He sealed his hopeless love in a roadless island

He couldn't find a way home to be with her

So he snuggled in the shadow of her love but his joy was short lived

If there was another life

I wish they'd build their home together

because the world was unkind to their love, forbidding them to be together

Remind me

If I break down over silly things...

Remind me that you will always be by my side and not run away

If I lose faith...

Remind me to put my trust in Him

If I turn myself down...

Remind me of my strongest day

If I fall apart....

Remind me how I pull myself back up

If I stop trying....

Remind me how far I have reach

If I lose hope....

Remind me why I started to fulfil the purpose of life

If I lost my way...

Remind me about the many roads i have ravel

I needed u....

But you walk away at my weakest day

I need him

Haunted vow

The fallen desolated house on the street

Makes me encounter lost for something I never even had

And makes me wondered alone

what are the memories that once took place inside of this or

How it came to be abandoned??

I was driven by

how the rest of the fallen pieces of wall and cranky front door

Still look as aesthetic as the rest of the town house

The rusty window bars still hold strong and in place

Yet sad and forbidding to enter the entry gate

The old palm tree in the front doorway seems calm but lonely

Wanting to tell the stories of it all

Before her leafs grow weary and wither in frozen weather

Many has talk about and passed by but never tries to listen

Solace and sorrow ravel in the air as I gazed

Unfolding the silence in the shadows of her leafs

seizing and witnessing the Truth in a luring ways

The moment was warm and distressed

Only to know

How fatal love can get??

And controlled the domain to be deserted

Felicities of togetherness is in its past

Life has gone to be never loved again

Horror and anxious blend in eternity of their vow

Adrift

He took a sip of white alcohol and his blackened heart sink deep in their cascade of love

The sad love song played on the radio remind him of how much he has loved a girl

A young love song but an old love story

That broke his heart to find another but never found one

Time and us

We once gaze the same moon

But now you are chasing shooting stars

When I still long for the same moon

Time spaces us

Would you?

Would you stay If i wasn't your first

Thingamphy horam

Stand by my side

Sun flared up and wood burn by the fireplace

Smoke overshadow the beauty of love

We are like a dying star that no longer fight for the gravity of love

But I can still see your teary eyes

We still have each other in our hearts

So stand by my side or we might lose the battle

Because together we have always thrive

Didn't know

Never knew

You'll endure the biggest scar

Never thought

You get the deepest cut

Never imagine

We will be apart to find ourselves

All at once

How wonderful it is to fall in love

How painful it is to lose

How hurtful it is to bid goodbye

Essences

What about you and me

What do I know
When everything I see and heard
Feels like thunder striking on my body
My emotion sink down to the dept
Have I been the victim of your sordid?

What about the late night conversation
That fill up the blank spaces between us
I once thought I will add live to it
With all shades of colour from violet to red
From Non-living to living words
But now my soul has been deserted,
So does the words

What about the friendships loyalty
Have I been playing hard all this time
Or has my sincerity been your check board game for this long
The world is bright and kind
But what about you and me

Can we

My friend

We both know

Sky's the limit

But the stars and the moon is just not enough for us

You set up land in favour beyond boundaries

And burnt your heart to be in my silence

The road to freedom and friendship lost traces of meaning

Your tender care that once fills my life now whispers afar

Not because I was careless,

But your intention was wrong

Can we just be real?

Thingamphy horam

Endless wall

It's been long gone

That I lose sight of what is right and what is wrong

The cruelty of times tore apart the fabric of friendship

Those once merry voices, now hover and echo in the wind faster than time

Greed and grudges threat the soundness to an extent

There was no sun, no star, no moon

Trap within an empty space

Existing with no contentment

'We' soon become 'I'

Fighting for pride that dire the moment and not to surrender

And every emitting words in vanquished.

we grow stiff and cold

Trying to see through the future in haze

And reckless spirits drives fast to go of off the cliff

With trembling voices mumbled thousand Go...... od byes

Building an endless wall between us

Bitter

Having a conversation with you is like a cup of hot sweet tea in my rainy days

Calm and warm

Not being aware of the stormy hurricane

That chained my emotion for your safer room

Note:Sweet talker not always sweet

Maybes

Maybe's and sometime's is a tricky game

They either lose you or you are stuck in the trap with bruises and unanswered question

The game is on

Faces

Your innocent ideas of life

Had my eyes open to believe in what I see, not in what i hear

Because authenticity is the key to find the true self

Living in your world of perfection to please others

Wrapping all the flaws and insecurity behind that sinister smile

Lure to prey warmth, you become your own victim of lies

Will this betrayal of anger humble you

Or has it become the root of your great lies

That follow the trail of twisted faults and sights

Is it worth practicing the silent act of brute

Note: Can we embrace authenticity

Ghost

Friends is what we are

Yet you kissed me

And hug me tight

Your first kiss was a trial

Your last hug is forever

Your smile and all the good words drifted into dawn

The walk we took in the moonlight is miles away and unspoken

The whole world mocked at us because we are just another friend

You stood up and

I followed you blindly

I walk bare the past days

You are like the ghost In person

Because you come and go when you want

My passion flamed up at dusk and

Wish let the memories fade away as the day

goes by

Every night your shadow yearned in my dream

I am the dream maker

without an owner

So look away,

I will not remember you

We are something that is not destined to be

Now promise me you will never come back again

Masquerade

Can you see with

Your eye mask on

Or you get comfortable being

blind folded

In a piece of black clothe

Thick and foggy

Invisible and irreversible

at times

Pretending to be real

and true

Trying to use someone else's

emotion as avaricious

As it can be

for your silver lining

And calling it

moving on.....

When you are still

Feeding your soul

From the past trash

There is no other way other

than to dispose him in

his past trash can

Delude

Tame me with that look

I can see

All your past

Deluding in your eyes

Shirtless man

Fast cars, clubs, whiskey and girls were his life

Time is never too late for him

But his age doesn't favour him

Now he is just another shirtless man that haunt his own age and spirit

Supper

You look at me like you want to devour me as your supper

Religious man

He spent time with her religiously,
man of great mind
Read her the words of faithful man from the Bible
But he never exhibit the man he admire

As much as he love "the parable of the prodigal son",
but he is a son who never find his home

He preaches like a priest
His voice echoes in sleeping night
Crunching the autumn leaves in sweet words,
trading her innocence vaingloriously
Twisting her thought in far end

Blurry vision of fear crushes trust into dust
Emotion too much for the body to take or words too much to express
Her spirit evaporates in different shapes and sizes,
Her body stays afloat through time and space
Delusion of his religiosity lured another woman or more.......

Drowned

He pour his insecurity in a glass of wine
and drowned himself in the glass with remorse
And asked me
Why don't you drink??
Why not try alcohol?

His unimaginative question makes me think secretly to myself....
We are in a beautiful place
We are young
There's music
We can dance a little
We are potentially capable of falling in love
Maybe we can kiss for the first time

There is so much more to share
A little laughter to feel comfortable on our own skin
Lying down beside each other to share our deepest desire for life
And stay up a little longer
Just because you find intoxication in our stories

Be strong

When he told me about love,I told him about life

When he told me about his past life,I told him how I would want to build my future

When he told me about the first time someone broke his heart,I told him about how the first time I fell in love

When he told me about unhealthy relationship with his ex's lovers, I told him how I am still working on my-self to be whole to love someone unconditionally

When he told me about all the wrong people he met,I told him about how I get inspired by every person I meet

When he told me about his unsuccessful career,I told him about my first job and the first pay check

When he told me about how he hated his dad,I told him about how my dad teaches me to love and forgive

When he told me how uncertainty of life always knocks him down,I told him how I grow Each time I face uncertainty in my life

When he told me about how to be soft and live in a certain ways to be a lady,I told him how lucky I am for not even close to be with a narcissist

Thingamphy horam

When he told me he need a strong woman to make him a strong man,

I told him.....to be with strong woman he need to be strong first

Be strong

Be strong

Be strong

And Be strong

The Brittle Ways

Wasn't it difficult to grow different kinds of flower at one time

Can two seasons occur at the same time and bestow upon the earth with finessing charm

Will we be there holding hands when the sun and moon eclipse, fighting over the world?

Won't your soul search for an assuring heart in the end

or is it in your nature to manage the complexity by dealing with different people at a time

Can trees give up its roots to bear branches of fruits

Can love grow ravenously ,spreading the root as far as the heart can bare the limits unseen

When

How much of his love has dipped you in pain

But you still choose to stay

Hoping love will change him someday

Note:That someday... when???

No one

No one would be able to love her enough to fill the hole within

For all her life, what she got from love is to be

wary, prudent, sensible, shrewd

When does loving someone has to go such extreme and beyond ourself to find the true and accurate meaning of love.

Peacock the pain

When the drop of rain touches the ground his feet are on move

fanning his train of feathers

Quivering and stretching his wings

High on flaunting a majestic look thinking he has someone to impress with his majestic tail

When peahen is busy raising their offspring alone and her plain tail

She looked at him in vain

And asked

when will you stop being a slave to your feather??

Wide road

She put a stone on his way for him to stumble upon

but the road he walks now is wider than her thoughts,
descending her stone into atom

Deceptive sip

When his anger rages

His body cripple

He hissed with his fist

Every time he breathes

His respiration weighed him down

His eyes turn creepy and black

His face scorned

He would throw his tantrum to everyone near him

Resentment and bitterness is the poison, the poison he inherited from his mother

Thingamphy horam

Foyer désuni

Who knows about broken home?

Only those

Who endure life from

A Broken soul

Reckless

Life pauses and hang
Moon grew darker
No one wept but tears fill ones eyes
The purpose is blurry in vision
And lost in the shadow of illusion

Life goes on.. so does time
Some People live in you just to fill their empty spaces
Hollow is their mind
Weaker is their emotion
They leave in a trail like a toxic wind

Life says, let it go....
But will it ?
when their shadow still wakes you in your sleep
contagious lies spill and spur in your heart
They are none..none other than reckless being

Possessed

Thingamphy horam

Collision of Dreams and responsibility

When our dreams and responsibility shakes with fear

The angst strangle us day and night

Every breath we take

Becomes a dagger piercing in the chest

when only the successful becomes the superior human and discriminate the failure as a failed games of life

Our goals become our demon that autocrats and confuse the world

And our head becomes the prison that is hard to release

And our minds get entangled with the fear of social denial

When we endure the complexity of expectation

Our shoulder weighs as heavy as a heart soaked in guilt

That cannot be soothe

And sans sin we dig our grave in darkness

Between live and life

While learning to live, we forget how precious life is

We are down on our knees pleading for love

because to live without love has become a sin

So, fear born fatigue and loneliness

We go by the rule and not strive

We often get confused with reel and real and forget how to act following the rules

Who will change before the world consume fully

Silence and modesty

We confuse them for weakness, some trade their sanity with insanity by the rule of dictates.

And their breath ceased trying to please before knowing their full potential of life.

And at what cost.

Voices of truth

We no longer hear or listen

Because we are bound by ignorant bliss

Only the brave to face the truth of life should listen to the melody of nature and become wiser

Beyond

The more we want, the more we lose

Our wants could go beyond

Our own capabilities

And create rooms for tribulation

The more we want, the more we lose grip of hope and ideas of living

So we often go on moping around

Not knowing where to start or end

Inanimate

We die living

We are doomed for wealth, beauty and standard

Where soul no longer has a place to survive

The breathe rod fear, rage and

enmity

Battling against ourselves

Seeking power and justice

The glittering eyes which once lit the stars are full of rue

There's no way but to free them

then,

life comes to end......

Cradle and grave, we mourn and dig

The daylight took us in and

The night descends with a sigh

Thingamphy horam

Shouldn't be

When power can take away ones life

And make them laugh on the wrong side of the mouth

I can see the bottomless abyss in their eyes,

those sleepless night, those eye bag hangs heavier than the weight of the mountain

those thoughtless bravery trade the innocence of peace and love

Aren't we ought to live our life

Our very existence in this world shouldn't be mistaken for power

Fear of dead

He says

He don't want immortality.

But the fear of dead

Lingers with His every breath.

How I wish

You were born immortal.

Better together

While counting the numbers of our age and mundane things

We stop counting the deeds we receive and give

A Blessing in disguise that comes like a flash in a gloomy days

Voices of forgiveness reaches the deaf to open their hearing

A little efforts of comfort brightens the world and turns the blind to open their eyes.

Fulfilling the need of others by giving a hand, an act of implanting seeds of felicity to forget the drunken might in us

Showers of Grace pours down in abundance to love others

inspiring and encouraging the withering soul

Those that we receive

Those that we reap

Those lives that we reach and touch will carry the harmony of peace

When are we going to realise that life is better when shared.

Together

Life gets easier

When we learn how to live by each other happiness

Graceless

A heart without grace is dry and empty

And this emptiness will turn into trepidation

then our conscience starts playing with fire

Breath by breath our soul burns into ashes

the destruction that brought down the stars from the galaxy has more glory than our demising soul

The Cigarette

The cigarette in your fingers burn like the pit of hades

The smoked flies in the air like cumulonimbus

Every footsteps filled with ashes

And whisper Damn! Let the past be gone

Your lips kisses its butt and inhale that very thing in your lung

It does sure give you a taste of paradise,

An aroma of nardos of valerian

Now you are on top of the world

How long will you disguise?

How long will your hallucinating mind own the world?

Come back

And face the reality of life

Thingamphy horam

Tainted Table

The family feast is full when grace is shared together.

But you place me in a distant branch of the bough

We were in the same roof but I was served in an odd table

Which makes me feel waif and not invited

I wasn't accepted as part of her family

The portion I swallowed choked my hoarse parched throat and

Some portion I couldn't still digest it,

though it's been two decades, it is still choking on my throat

Because you didn't give me space to sprout my branches from the bough

Shadow

Sometime our own shadow become our enemy that hurt us even when our enemy cannot

Think of me

The next time when you look up the sky and see those glimmering stars

Think of me

For I am thankful and embracing myself among the stars for all the degraded words you said and the be-littling wounds you left for my unsuccessful career.

Your words couldn't consumed me but burn down my thousand failures

So and So

Some people just roll in your life to mess things up and denigrate you

My Sunshine

You are treasured and valued
beyond numbers
I cherish you all for all that
you are to me

Thingamphy horam

My guide

In my mess, I am the angel in his eyes, heaven smells like the flowers from his garden

The bliss in my heart spur over by his kindness

Contentment and wholeness locked austerity of his life

He chose to listen the most undesired story,

His teary eyes ignites in ever ending flames

Makes the most dangerous decision,

spring sprung in his bravery and breeze in the trees sing along with his honesty

He journeyed through the longest day and the darkest night,

sometimes the sun sank in the coldness of the dark clouds,

the stars folded behind the sky, where the moon buried face....

He still says, my baby, don't be afraid of the steep Mountains and Brutal river wide,I will always be your guide,

He paints my world with compassion

In the end. He says, more love, more sacrifices, more giving, more happiness....

Against all odds in his body and soul, and hardest task of all the things

He knows one thing "Hope", hope can melt the frosty days and revive his strength like that of sunrise and make him rise above the soaring mountains

He hid his sweats and tears under a smile that shape every bit of I am, his pain carve in my body forever.

My Father knows less about the world but his experience has taught me everything about life,

There will never be enough time to be in his arms..

Nail paint

Pink is never my colour

But pink nail paint is the most enchanting nail colour I have ever received as a gift from Papa when I was six

The nail cutter was too blunt to cut my nail yet his patience never dies

He scrubs my nail with a rusted filer like the Craftsman grace his work with fine things that efface the edges

He painted my nail elegantly

And drew the way through the milky ways to give me the universe and the galaxies

He drew stories of life on my little fingers, prolonging the rare perfection of fathers-daughter moment

Papa is the mirror of life and the essence of love that contains full of grace

Pink is never my colour but the nail paint is my favourite thing

Taste

Papa and I attended a cousin's wedding.

After the ceremony

Papa took me to a small shop at the corner of a street and

Bought me two chocolates

The sweetness reminds me of his taste on chocolates

Thingamphy horam

Map for destination

You are the face of my life

Your silent prayers keeps me safe

When my feet are cold

I can feel your blistered feet rubbing to warm my feet

Your smile reminds me of your fearless face

Your tears are my shield

In your words I find treasure

Journey of my life starts in your wisdom

As I take the journey of life

The best route to reach my destination is in your map

'My mother map for destination'

I walk down the lane with fear

Your footsteps awaited me

I walked along and discover the beauty of the world

The world tries to take me away, away in the wrong direction

But today, I've discover a bare feet with crack in the heel

A fresh blood stain on the ground

Footstep of love, care and sacrifice

They strive me each day to live on....

Thingamphy horam

Mama

Mama sings like a bird

Dances like the waves

Sway with the wind

Mama cries a river

bend and break many times

She sweats an ocean

Mama runs deep within the valley

Shook the mighty mountain

She prayed numbers of sand in her sleepless night

Mama aged is cruel yet she is still kind

She stumbles at times yet she selflessly love and

She showed me the strength of a woman

Thingamphy horam

She is a farmer

The sun is drowning

The rainstorm sings

Mama laid on the side of the bed

She has been unwell for the past week

But we couldn't take her for treatment as

The virus messes dragoon into rife

She couldn't be at the farm for a while now

Her mind is anguished as she thinks about the seeds she sowed

The Wild fury grasses devours

While she prays for more sunshine

I could imagine the wieldy and yielded hand

The stiff leg and blistered feet benumb by the cold misty fog

Her stained clothes hanging on the verandah overseeing the farm, her spade and basket are parched

Lying on the floor to satiate their thirst

In her mind

she was battling with her health

and the weeds in our farm

Her heart live in the soil

she find solace in a grimy toil

She is a farmer who taught me not to be contrite of my tarnished hand

So I pick up her spade and the basket to toil and moil

Humbling

How humbling it is to sleep on the floor

With a bedsheet that mama stitches from pieces of clothes

How humbling it is to grow food on the farm

To know that it takes to fill the yawning stomach

How humbling it is to see shoes covered with holes and dirt

We groan and pant, then we grin balancing the basket full of vegetables on our head

How humbling it is to experience our clothes drenched with sweat

Detached from the noises and chaos from the madding crowd, with hearts full of gratuity while gazing and listening at the green lush caressing by the soft breeze to revive the spirit of gratefulness.

To my Grandmother

When love took you home and turn away in words

Your motherly womb gave me a mother who give me life

When beauty is the thing

You give me the world beyond grave

When your untainted heart throbs with the silence you put to everything they say

You created me a heaven in my sleepless night

When you dealt with adversities and disappointment

You show me the bright side of life

When your body drowned in the weight of responsibilities

Your strength showed me how to swim over the side of the shore sand

When I thought love is an affair,

You pray with me and ask God to bless me with a good man

When the scar in your hands and blue veins in your skin taint

You uphold like a tree stretching its arms reaching towards all the tired branches

When your back feels like nails drilling against your bone

You show me the beauty and joy of mother and a grandmother

Thingamphy horam

Motherhood

All things wither away

But the love of a Mother and

The Beauty of Motherhood remains the same

Love and forgiveness

Papa taught me how to love

And mama taught me how to forgive

So that I can always love and forgive

Let love and forgiveness be always my way

Thingamphy horam

Forgiveness without price

My father was at his late 60s

When he was beaten by a group of men

as a punishment based on

customary law

because he was too outspoken

to the man

I saw in the pulpit

as a preacher and a pastor in the church

When I was a little girl

Wondering away by the faith of humanity treacherously,

His forgiveness lies in bending my father's body on the floor of his house

Where all the young man put their fist on his flesh

My maternal uncle told me that

He was assaulted about ten times,

But the number was more

Father pleading of guilt was heard and witnessed by those elderly man from the clan

Who watched him without showing mercy

How does a house of prayer sounds when a faith of good shepherd

Question a wasted words

Mother put questions

Did he deserved to be beaten at this age??

Is there no better way to pay the cause?

She mumbled eivasha, eiposha.......

My heart wrenched when she cried

It was hard for me to convince

the world of separation that bound the dignity of a person's worth

on raising a hand on elderly man

One day may his soul carries my father's quilt in his grave yard

And the mark of my father's bruises in heaven

There we shall remember only the good times

There, May the forgiveness lies without a price

Thingamphy horam

Life or them

From the beginning towards the end

Engraving love at the edge

Ocean roar, when you cry silently.

Who do we blame?

Life or them

You have been torment by their ages voice

You have been torn apart by their cruelty

You have been mentally disturbed by their ego

You have been a maid to protect their loyalty

You have been burning for their pride

You have become the beast by their jealousy

Who do we blame?

Life or them

They cursed you

They stoned you

They changes God's name into theirs

Thingamphy horam

Word

My brother and I live by words

We have no better way out the chaos inside our mind

We comfort each other by silly laughter

Support each other with kind words

And eventually every action turn into words

When we have no other way than to live by words....

Words are home and peace for us

Thingamphy horam

Dawn of our childhood

Sound of the rain pattering on the tin roof is a lullaby

we long to sleep with when we are far away from home

The cozy smoky fire place is the haven, where we took our first step, the dawn of our childhood and here we learn the value of family

Dusty flake that flies around in the hair spinning in infinite to unwrapped our dreams to let it fly high

We crowd like those pop corn popping around one after another looking out the misty mountain through the unparalleled window, diving at the bottom of the sea, a life full of mysterious journey

At the four corner of this home, father recites the prayers for our journey

Those wall raised in happiness, with love the windows gleam

and the sun ray glow with us

This old home taught me to stand tall with glory and gives me timeless moment to form a constellation above the horizon

Time's and memories

Waking up at 4 am, not getting enough sleep

I was aimlessly drifting and lonely

I closed my eyes and smile wistfully recalling some of the lullabies sang to me by my grandma when I was a kid

And Bed time stories of those courageous warriors, "Maro the orphanage boy",........

My heart goes out for the poor boy

So,I promised grandma I will love the needy and the loner,

she would bade me good night, baby rest the night with warm and in peace

I am wide awake struggling for deep sleep

Humming those lullabies and whispering the stories in silence to myself

But doesn't make me any easier

So, I thought I am not sighing myself away with this unpleasant, sleepless night

But will remember how I pampered myself with memories

And those stories every kid in town wish to hear from my grandma

Then,I realised I haven't talk to her for a month

Time and memories bring us closer

in a sleepless night

Haunting Rhythm

You'll forget the sun in this jealous rain as they pour on the tin roof....

This morning I kept humming with the unforgettable haunting rhythm of childhood rain.....

Thingamphy horam

Footprint

The Misty mountains
The cold water
Those Frozen grass
The Air from the bow
The Warm fire place
Will they wait for me?

Where love is shared
Tales that live in thy heart
The promises made within families and friends
Laughter that wake streams and rivers
The thoughts from our deepest mind
And believing from heart touches historic peak
That our footprint will stay there
For years and years.

Her mother

O' Mother, your ways aren't always paved with golden path

But the presence of your zeal affectionate the nature to flare up like an igniting flame and gave me a home of kindness

O' Mother, your prayers shielded me when my spirits are low

At dawn, Your discreet homage to church makes you the guardian angel I've heard of

And the humble pleas you chant gives me the strength to go on

O' Mother, who refine your patience and your femininity

Your smiles and laughters are slowly making its gleamy mark on the milky ways

The universe you breathe is a tick away

O' Mother, whose creation are you

And who am I to deserve your motherly love that stops the trembling globe

Your love has me gaze at the vast sky to explore your divine heart

Thingamphy horam

New path

We once felt winter was eternity

Drenched in worries and stress, that was the dream we thought we dreamt of

And broken relationship of our love ones folded in our heart like a love letter of sadness

they were as cold as ice upon the memories of angers and hatred

But we buried tears that was turned blue hue under the bonfire in the campsite

By the crack of the firewood....

we broke the silence of injustice done by this world

And by rushing of the river we bade goodbyes to our past

The skies become our roof

those countless stars sings the anthem of friendship

Where moon lead us to the road of new path

Promised land

As long as there is breathe in me and before the sacrament water anoint my body

The sweet voice of my grandchildren will not go in silence

The calm and warm air in this house will narrate the stories of love and hardships.

Then my heart will be content like there's no limit beyond those bondage

My shoulder will be there for them to rest on .... until all of us drifted off beyond the horizontal valley.

May the celestial breeze welcome us with its elixir of memories and cleanse our soul when we reach the promised land.

Power

So grateful to you for giving me the power to fly the coop

Note: To my parents

Sprouting with Season

Spring

spring arrives with new shoots and charm the departing hills

Those flora and fauna dances a little longer with the joy of being alive

Birds came along, romanticising the coming of spring

The Queen of the mountains visit in her finest robe

Crimson wings and velvet ring

Golden palace, her presence resonate as she vibrate

The flowers and its bud fall in her hypnotic nature

She pollinate and bring bountiful harvest

Her buzzing nature solemnise each with her affection

Spring brought us a journey bigger than you and i

To conquer the cosmos and the universe deep within

As we travel with spring

we shall live beyond this body and mind to triumph our own existence

Spring and herself

Spring sprung and has brought amenity of its beauty

The breeze somewhere

so untouched and isolated

that it feels like you are the only one in the planet

Even the aimless wild flowers is elegant and cinematic as the warm wind waft around them

They soothe the soul and heighten the consciousness of her femininity

which makes her feel precious at once.....

And adorning herself with tender love and care

Reminding her to nourish herself to flourish with spring,

though the errand of season might soon take her away

Thingamphy horam

Oh Moon

Oh Moon! Aren't you tired to come out every night

How many more secrets will you listen to?

Aren't you tired of gazing down on the barren slopes and height?

Do you still see euphoria in them.

Oh Moon! Aren't you tired of hearing wishes over and over again made by drained souls...

Will you still listen to the silence once more?

Aren't you tired of holding the words together from falling apart?

Oh Moon! Don't you get anxious when sun replace you..

Aren't your nature of calmness that travel the endless path

Won't you pave the way for the tender and dying souls?

Oh Moon !

Astrophile

Though,

I am not a sabaism

My soul live longer at night

And my eyes shall linger

Till sunrise

Scribbles

I walk passed a busy market

And bought a warm pair of socks, some fudgy brownies and chocolates

for the late night scribbles

At Midnight, the lamp glows tenderly as I scribble

each word I scribbles melt along with the warm brownies.

The pair of socks keeps me warmth enough to see the sunlight before I snuggle in my bed of fleeting dreams

Scribbling kept me up

That Shy guy

I giggle and dream's

About the dreamy shy guy in the café

I am way too old fashion

Not to do anything rather than smile back at stranger

Even, though his smile held me a-gaze

Long enough to be cheeky

Humility

Just like the sea meets the sand

Your simplicity and humility

Meets the heart of a dreamer

Moment

A cup of hot reviving brew on the right,

A book on the left

The dew filled window,

And the burning coal

Each words comes to life and every moment cherished

Paradise

Your path is more similar to eternity

I go naked and barefoot

with your innocence

for innocence could be the home of paradise

November crush

Be kind to me

I will remember you

Treat me well

Let me love you

Smile for me

I will warm your heart

Say you love me

I will never leave you

Watch me

I will never let you down

Hold my hand

I will let my hand fit into yours

Show me

I will feel you

Cover me up

I will let you inside me

Discover me

I will let you taste the real me

Tell me I am amazing

I will do magic for you

Tell me you breath for me

I will make memories for the rest of your life

In hush

It was as good as time

And the night turns gay

When I heard him singing from afar

Oh! He could crush me with his voice! I mumbled and leaped

into the crowd to cheer for him

He sounds like a Ney

And his eyes, as beautiful as the pearl of the south sea

His hand are soft yet rough at the same time

When he asked my name

My word spills and my mind chanting to know him more

We frame the moment in picture

My heart has the delicacy of lace

And it's as intricate as the pattern of my brain

He crushed me in a hush

She is one

She asked me
Why do you have so much of love and connection with people?
Is it from your mother
Or from your daughter?
She asked again,

I smiled and told her
I am footloose and fancy free
But, if I have a daughter
I will make sure
She lay her head on my chest every single day
Her home is where I am

Her eyes shimmered with tears,
That tells me
Human spirits are both fragile
And magnificent
And she is one
Note: to the stranger, we become friends

Path of life

She walk through paths of life
That, she fold all the elements
Of her life in her ageing skin
My heart wounded for the causes

Learning stories of her life
I was making a cenemic reality scene in my head
Picturing image of agony and despair
Dialogue of rejection and desolation
Music of griefs and of struggles
Action of kindness and sacrifices
Places from her past,
Past to present, present to future
She had lived and live in plot of colours

It sounds horrific
But, We were flooding in infinite Galaxy of stories
We learn each other passionately in a joyful tears
I found magic in her heart and there
She won the trophy of life.

Her heartbreak

She told me how love ached her once fierce heart

As I listened to her without saying a word
She ran out of words .

I can only feel her heart slipping in deeper agony..

Her custom

Grandmother from that old town

Once told me

You need to understand the culture before you understand a man

But what if one understands a man's soul better than his culture

Will their be reverberation of unaccustomed hate on her innocent love

??????

When you

Asked me

How it's like

To be a woman

All I could say was

How does it feels

to be

A son?

Abundance

She craves for lemon
Then, chilli pickle

Later on
She ask for cucumber salad

Little did I know
she has life inside of her

Now I can't wait for
the beautiful soul to see the world

Coin

So you said, I am a natural romantic

That is tempting me to invent

destiny

Thingamphy horam

Sea of life

The sea waves swivel tenderly and sensuously

loner left their despair in the breezy soft sand,

water haul to dig beneath the deepest depth

And the silence of the clear blue break their chain in proper purity

The tides are low and the air refreshes the ambience

Bikini ladies embrace frolicked in the sand

Like Queen of the sea, mermaid murmured in envy of your beauty

Couple in their mid 70's

Breathing love and sharing laughter

Sailing in their memories of boat

Keeping promises in endless summer

Fisherman unhooking his fishing boat,

Sailing across the ocean while

The sun mark his brown skinny skin, moulding his every stroke of Oar into perfection

His spirit lift along with the rise of the tide

Knowing his love ones await for platelets

A kid with his garbage bag hanging on his shoulder, with big dreams in his eyes

A heavy rock gilded in his feet but looking towards the sky to reach his goal

My breathe catches the beauty of the sea

And painted my mind in the sea of life

Then Suddenly the wave got wild

And flow back and forth

Like the sun knows it's for setting

So I leave with the sunset in awe

Grateful

Grateful for the unpromised breathe

Graceful morning aurora landed softly on the window panes

New city smells like the perfume wear by your imaginary man

Sidewalk makes you feel a lot like home

Grateful for all the Little things

seeing a kid licking the ice cream pouch clean

Seeing a stranger starting a new book in the sub way

An old woman embracing her pale grey hair and tottering in the yard to soaked the warm sun

A mother breastfeeding her baby at the Corner of the concrete building to calm her cry

Grateful for the Gracious lives

The Lady at the airport in her wheelchair was kind enough to give a hand despite of her difficulties, her act reflects her life's journey

Your first hello to the strangers will probably become the last hello but their humility remain in your heart and soften your view of the world in many ways

Grateful for the moment
Riding an old fashion yellow taxi,
Rain dazzling on the windshield makes you remember the bittersweet tears once shed
Visiting a historical monument alone, those sculpture too dramatic that you want to be their theme

Grateful for the Seasons
An empty street filled by little twinkling Christmas spirits bring closer to your love ones and memories of loss, hurt and hope amended
Waiting for a gift of hopeful new year which will release some undeterred pain and welcome in new winds and new days

Grateful for all the denials
Thanking in pillow to those who treat you as their maybes....... Not just a profound life lesson but makes you realise your worth
Waiting for thousand prayer to be answer
Tapping into compassion and learning how to be more patience

Contentment

The rocks rambles on their own way and fits in wherever they landed

They do not worry about how much space they own and

how much more space they'll need to make a home

This contentment makes life much more contented

Grasses are standing tall,

even if they ripple among the winds

They are carefree and ready to face the uncertainty

that crushes and bend them and

spread seeds wherever the wind blows

The crashing waves looks wild

yet it is a reminder of disparity, brokenness, fear

that makes up different layers to rise as high to blind the sun

the moment we trust our inner self

We clothe ourselves with strength as we rise.

My soul and the whole world

People know you for being Solitary

But it's pleasing and mysterious

Watching the sunset with the melody of birds singing

Waking up the next morning

With a carefree mind

Untie your fairy boat

And row over to the place

Where you have never been,

Call the wild breeze and curve the stone

Your life can be as aesthetic as Caspar David Friedrich

Wherever you go

Imagine, watching the sunrise in the east coast

Playing your fave music

Sometimes, It's okay to ride your bicycle

On the clouds.

I am living my present life

without a gap with nature

Why would I be afraid of being alone?

When I own my soul and the whole world

Sailor

I am a sailor in the sea

With a broken boat and a wrecked heart

I strive to explore every little detailing imprinted in my journey

I yearn to unravel my destiny in my sail

I have love the old and new

I believe in living and transposing into dust

I want to experience all seasons.

With the coming of storm, I see the tiny boats rowing towards the shore hurriedly

And with the storm abates, the sea bade my hair to reach for the light

I am to work and gain humility beyond life

I am to catch every wind, my canvas encounters in my sail

The idea to dream, to explore and to live keeps my heart flutters

I cannot fathom the idea of bounded living.

Because, I am a dreamer of wonders

Watering

Morning dew

When the silence of the night makes me awake

My mind walk through the

forest

And wait for the morning dew

To shower my soul

Your ocean

If the world was made for us

Will you still sink in the depth of your obscure perplexed thought

And keep me dripping in your ocean

where the waves you created crest on my innocence

If I can be your tears

I will let it seep into the soil

just to nourish and keep one flower alive

And let her own the sunlight,

convert her beauty into hope

To let her bloom in changing seasons

So that she will not be wither and swept away by the cruelty of swinging seasons.

Thingamphy horam

The truth

Truth is the only way to set us free from this chaos

And your eyes speaks the language of truth

Now release me from the shadow of your enchanting secrets

One shouldn't crawl for being truthful

What if

What is love?

If love has condition

What if,

Love has to only received, not to give unconditionally

What if,

Love subjugate and closed a heart for intimacy

What if,

Love does not overcome fear, mistrust, guilt and loneliness

What if,

Love feels like a servant and not embrace freedom

What if,

Love feels like Evanescence and not a perennial realm

What if,

Love only compete and not favour other's love

What if,

Love value obedience more than relationship

What if,

Love is to succeed, not promising or take an oath

What is love?

If "what if" has all the phases of love

For I know

"Love is the greatest"

Of all.

Aura

She curled up and frowned

Wasn't it enough of the pale moon to mock at her fear???

Wasn't the night that kept her awake was too long?

When Sunlight touches her under eye bag and render her blind, encircling it like a stamp of unfriendly shadow

She curse herself for being bruised and torn

She unfurl and retrace

While she lay herself on the bed silently ,as if not to daunt by her heavy breathe she takes

She wants to blow away her pain to restore her aura and fill her soul with love and beauty

In her winter of garden

In her winter of garden

Birds migrate and chirps in silence

It's soothing, it's soaring

During winter, she soar a high

In her winter of garden

flowers unwind to rest on the ground blinded by the sun covering the garden floor

she finds the way of her eternal home

In her winter of garden

Her soul bloom under the moonlight with divine love

She listens to the whisper of the winds

Joyously her feet glide and in an exquisite sight, she traverse with the moon

In her winter of garden

peace and stillness rule

And break the chains of ferocity

During winter, silence falls to make amends and does her heart mend.

Process and healing

What a year I have been

I couldn't ask for more.....

Glimpse beyond life and the unseen, unfailing Divine love

Those healing tears I spilled are growth from within

I shall never forget thee

A hell and the heaven on Earth

I smile to all for all with love and forgiveness

The days and the year will end soon

In this passing time, bolder, yet soft like the lining from the clouds to shines through in new ages

My feet might stumble and

My body will not sustain this old soul forever

But I still have dreams to live on ...

And I long to live a profound life that will spur goodness among others

The rainbow after the rain

As I watched the rain drops on the translucent bulb hanging on the front porch

Each drop slips and down they went

Reminding me of my every crystal tears that once flows on my cheek

The tears I had endured together with a piece of tissue paper which has soothe my miseries gently,

And the stain on the pillow case,

The unending long night of loneliness where the difference of the world and dreams set to flames

and the dawn never awakes giving the reign to darkness

Becomes powerful keeping me away from everybody

If the tears I had shed had colours

You'd see rainbows on my cheeks and the stories of how I break the cycle of life where it hadn't been easy

Where I set my anger free that blue night and shut the voices that screamed 'you are too worthless to have dreams'

How heartbreaks and rejection gave me back the stolen trust I withdrew selflessly for long time

And the story of how I discovered my worth and feelings that has made me "Me".

It's the rain and the mud which gave me the sunshine and the rainbow more worthwhile

Hell fire

When we were together

I was in hellfire

Now that you are gone

The tip of my tongue

Feel the taste of Holy water

Now, all I need is redemption

Redemption To self, myself

Note:

Thank you for leaving me

For I have found peace

The peace I have never experience

Differences

When you came back for the second time

You had me known the differences

Between to know ones worth

And to fall for you again

May you know how much of your lies has consoled me to stay away from you

So I had to leave knowing my worth

Unwanted

The very last time I think of you was

Couple of years ago

I was the sky line in your cheek bone

Living in the height of skyscraper

You were reaching the moon

And counting the stars in your fingers like playing piano

But, now your heart is an empty living shell in an abandon coast

Which could no longer clench the forces from the vast deep ocean

So the waves washes you away

And Landed on sand, sun-baked and unsecured

Bounded by millions of tiny little shell

Unwanted

Thingamphy horam

Two line

I try to write down all the words you said
And put all the words together in two line

"You are still living in yesterday"
"Tomorrow seems too far for you"

Tuck all the memories in the past
And kiss them away before the silver moon disappear

Then, You will live today with no regrets
Because tomorrow is here

He and his perfection

He said, I am the rose that bloom with a crooked stem

Of all my imperfection I will still be beautiful
as I am

Of all your perfection I hope you find a cure for your
insecurity

Thingamphy horam

Faded seasons

In the wake of Spring, he asked what her name is

Reciting her all the sweet sonnets

Like he was nurturing the rose in the sacred garden of Eden

In summer he took her out to see the sunrise

They took the isle of boulevard

Beneath the blue untainted sky

Paved with unearthly emerald sand

The straying clouds wander by...a promise land are to be discovered, he whispered

In Autumn, he made her tea before the falling leaves

With a smile as humble as the leaves dying

Without a thought or time she sat upon his heart

As time went by they still talk about that one summer sky

In winter, he vanished

Absconded along with the cold winter wind

She watched each fading sunset drowned behind the same mountains they once wish upon

The golden ray on the grey leaves reminds her of his dying love

In deep woods, she laid his fading love beneath the shade of starry night sky

Your peace

If life is a dream

I'll never wake you up

Cause your peace is all it matters

Time

When I am sad

I live in three different time

Past, present and future

Everywhere

Where does the word live?

In my heart?

In my mind?

Every where in a void

To be whole

Take your time

Moving on is not about

How quickly you move on

How much time it takes

Moving on is

about uplifting and

Helping ourself to stretch our wings

Take a break

until you set yourself free from

Tormentous, ruptured heart

Thingamphy horam

Every too

Too sensitive, too insecure

Too honest, too loud

Too loved, too cold

Too bold, too timid

Too generous, too selfless

The world is every too

When you don't find yourself

Budding

One minute

One minute of meeting you,

Can be a minute of everything

Never be more and less, when one minute can stop the world

Two way street

Can a man be

confident yet humble,

Gregarious yet loyal

Passionate yet gentle

And not victimising her

For being compassionate

Friendship should be a two way street one should never weight the emotional trauma of a victim

To winning trust,

To Winning acceptance and

To winning efforts

Thingamphy horam

Voices

If those voices reach my father's ear...

He will be heartbroken

because he didn't raise me that way

Sometimes words can be cruel and bribe your value

but I won't trade them

All i got to do is keep my calm to let the storm settle

Bouquet of flower

Thinking what it will be like to go out for coffee with you is wondering how spring is like in mars

So I pick up a bouquet of flowers and walk home to be in my world again

Three man in my dream

The First

Like we are ne'er destined to say a-yo again

We estranged and buried all the memories in the dome of your family's detestation

And you were still the same in my dream to the new girl

My heart breaks for her and my lips mumbled thousand prayers to give you faith in love.

The Second

Just like the way you came

You were aimlessly roaming in crowded streets

Disowning the Beauteous life around you

Losing track and trace, filling the gaps from a hell-brewed drink

My heart twinge in waking of my dream

The third

How I yen you to be as authentic as the way you were in my dream

Asking me to wait for two more years

And with promises of changes in your character

Your self doubt and pride detached us from reality of life

May it only be to the truth, truth the Excellency.

Castle

She know how to build a castle out of the things that almost crash her

Midnight tête-à-tête

He is with his mom and his granny, I don't know what kept them up till midnight or maybe I will never get to know

they must have been talking about how life has been for them

And here I am, dreaming about how I wish to be with my love ones, sitting near the fire place, a warm cup of tea in my hand, Grandma rubbing my back and talking all out from our heart

how we misses each other, giggles and endless talk of tales long gone like there's no tomorrow

He told me about how beautiful the starry sky look at home tonight

Like he knows stars, moon and the skies are my mys-tery

I would have walk miles in cold winter breeze, count the stars and keeping them in my palm or

Gaze to seek the sight from my window and cease my breathe to begin the story of how my soul roam among the stars with desire to find it's meaning

And ask how long will she stay?

Probably she'll mumble...... the moment you learn how to walk in lightless streets with glittering faith from the sky....

Thingamphy horam

Petal

Roses are in full bloom at the garden,

they are beautiful and ferocious yet fragile

And as I gaze them, each Petal tells a different story.....

Some save for the bees

Some nipped away by the butterflies

Some has bruises from the predators

Some never leave the butt until it get dried up by the sun

Some fall on the ground, when they couldn't hold the weight of the rain

Some has been rip from the root and are in someone's vase now

Some couldn't last for a day because they fall at the dark place

Some are still repenting their stem that has been stomped and bend by the wonderers

Some still yearns for more sun.............

Which Petal are you if you were a rose?

Thingamphy horam

She

She is beautiful and I'm insane

The bird sang their chant, for she is as mysterious as the sky

Seasons embodied to seek and learn her leniency towards lives

Every drop of tears remembered the art of struggle and victory she embraced in her delicacy

Days might fall short to keep her smile but she is the piece of stories they tell to the whole universe

Her nobility convinced the world that one's soul can be immortal

Her brokenness knitted all the broken pieces into love

Love is something she has nurtured with patient and not to conquer

And she is beautiful when she waits and trusts God's patient work in her

She is beautiful and I'm insane

I'll

I woke up when January ended

The days only lived, weeks dies upon the month

Wintry wind is cold enough to faint my lips

My cheeks are cool, my eyes pale

But my heart is warm and tender to spell love

May my soul always spur in forgiveness

Let the shadows of resentment dissolve in the air

For my prayers He will hear

My prayers He will answer

I guard my heart not to awe and for pride, but to be true and honour his timing

Refine my heart into a heart of gold,

It won't woe in charms and in evils

For I gladly surrender my whole into your flawless grace

I will recite the rhyme of all the many blessings and mercies among the golden leafs,

My feet will dance among the breeze for I have found myself

In your rhythm my heart beats firm and still

I'll kiss in thy faithfulness

When the first winter rain shower upon my skin

Slow down

Will you slow down

To find your way.

It's hard to get accepted

When you are moving too fast

The sky doesn't race always

Sometimes the desolated road doesn't always look that bleak

Such a craggy road it is....

but you are enough

life surrounds you the moment you find your inner soul

Life is too short not to love

Violence

Age can be a violence to our peace of mind

When one only counts and adds the number each year

In fact,

Ageing is a sign of knowledge and experience,

Knowing oneself is growing each and every second of life..

The universe of life has so much to offer you

Stop counting and start living

Beauty within wrinkles

Youngness might go away in a heartbeat but the beauty that lies within the wrinkled skin are uncountable tales

And I felt it all at once

Joy

Agony

Fear

Love

Lust

Firmness

Frailty

Agitation

Hatred

Death

The deeper it goes the sweeter our soul shall rest within those wrinkles

Mortal

The ticking age and the tides of time has shown me

How short our life is

A tale

He once told me a tale

Women are as wispy as flower

And it goes on and on.......

Little did he know

All his delicacies are just a scent of her

She is more than what you see

And what you wanted her to be

Flaws

Daisies,

Lilies,

Roses

A Beautiful thing

But

Covering up all your flaws with those flowers doesn't change anything.....

Instead,

Let all the impractical and unwanted scraps of life fertilise and nourish for growth to be you all over again

And be adorned like that of flowers

Perfection

Flaws aren't for imperfection

They are for perfection

Glow

Oh Darling,

Self care is not a crime
Keep nourishing to glow in your own way

Stay you

Fathom out by oneself is better than

Relying on someone else

All this

Some days, I am lost

Some days, I am broken

Some days, I am sad

Some days, I want to die

Some days, I lie on the bed starring at the ceiling thinking how blessed I am.

I am a fusion of all this

Thingamphy horam

On the road

Lone Adventure of life

Could be in a snowy road

Under a raging sun

On a rainy cloud

With a windy storm

You have to walk

Miles and miles

And learn to live

Life with it

Happiness is on the road,

Not at the end of the road

Bouquet of daffodils

Meet me halfway

Are u a dreamer??

If yes, meet me by the brook beyond those ridge
We can talk about our wildest dream

LOVE

The Wind that blows may eventually cease like us
Love shouldn't be just feelings but it should be seen in action
So Love unuttered and that is a love wasted

Losing in a way welcome new adventures
Heart that has been struck by emotion
will mean a world to someone someday

When you tell all the hardship of the past relationship
he will hold your hand tighter and notice the glimmering passion in your eyes
And wrap you up in a hug tight
That can only describe one thing:
LOVE

Frame

You be my word and I'll be

your art

Together

we'll frame the world

Thingamphy horam

To the love

They say

Let love guide your soul

But,

I will

Let my soul

guide

To the hearts, that has been broken,

To the hearts, that has never fallen in love

To the hearts, who has lost their lovers

To the unsung hearts and

To the skinny love,

yet

To say 'I love you'

Live by soul that leads to love

Honest

When everyone else talk about quality men...I dream of an honest soul...

Constant

I might not know what love is

But I know where my heart stands

Inseparable

Love is the beginning of life,

Life should end with love

Lucid

Love is not,

Lust is blind

Thingamphy horam

Hope and faith

Year is frozen, daylight is short

Mind is awake in the coldness

Tears are flaking in season of winter

White is beautiful

But not so,

When every part of you is bleeding

Counting on the last gasp of the breath

Knowing

If I blink it may cease to exist

That comes to the point

Life is real and worth fighting for

Seasons may not be favoured

But you are and I am

By moving of the wind

And light from the sunrise

Harvesting a basket full of ripened hope

Faith setting higher in glory

I shall make it

Because thou art great

Universe

Show me all the frail parts of you

That you don't love

So I know where to start

I'll reassemble all those part in a way

I have crafted my broken pieces and created a universe called home inside of me

Assurance

I was lost

I thought I'll never find a home

But the moment I met you

I knew you are my home

Thingamphy horam

Survivor

Fill me with love

Before the world drain in a hollow mind

Feed me with kindness

I am a survivor in your soul

Even when my head swim in an empty pond

My eyes will see the sunrise in your world

Spring will pass and fate will destine me in season

But I will flourish in your cherry tree

Fly

The world between us

gave us the world within us

and that is the space

where the light comes in

and we followed the light toward each other with broken wings

Our love is strong enough to hold us together....this time we fly without wings

Thingamphy horam

Get crazy

We can laugh until we cry,

stay until we die

We know spring gave us a crazy hay fever yet

we know love get crazy in the wildest of our blossom heart

Many years more

As long as there is love, dead cannot separate us

It has open the gate of eternal comfort

Each breath we take is a scripture written beyond the sky

When your eyes resembles the purest form of love

My face illuminates with joy

when you smile at me

My heart hums the rhythm of love

May our soul and body remains wholly in his arms

May our love taste purer than the finest pine honey from the west coast

And when the time comes, we may say "cheers" for many more years.

Loving you

The eyes that meet

The heart that stays

We'll see the smile in each other's eye

Love doesn't have to be perfect

As long as we are together

There's no now nor forever

Because I know life that live longer than numbers

"loving you"

Answer

My thoughts might run dry
And smile might go off someday
But when you are with me
I feel the rhythm in your laughter
I hear poetry in your words

Our stories might not make it into a love story book
We will not fall in love again to love another
because in your eyes I see forever
The look in you eyes gives me a promise of thousand stars

My morning shines brighter
When you kiss my forehead and talk about your favourite book
How your mama smile

Your grandma favourite dish recipe
And how your daddy like his tea.

Darling you are the answer to be in love

Love should look good

Love has change your perception of life

Love has make you whole

Love has make you a lot happier

Love does looks good on you

Tide of victory

How can we not be Happy for everyone

When beauty is a thing that live beyond life

Beauty is when you are still breathing,

When you are still moving,

Where there is still hope

Beauty is being someone, when there is no one

Beauty is the eye

Who watches above the clouds and across the sky

Beauty is kind, who learns to meet humility

Beauty is a tide of victory

Little things

When the world turns you down. Don't deflect it in false perception. Instead, get on your knees and count all the beauty in little things that life is offering you

How not

How not to dream of you at night, when its

strange to dream of you even when I am wide awake

Yet to meet

Slow down and feel the little things around you

Give all that you know and take in all what you need

I am on my way to meet you someday

May that someday reward us with the meaning of waiting

May you fulfil your dreams and love what you do

May you also meet new people along the way

But I hope you won't give away your heart away to them

Know that every dawn and dusk

My mind doesn't stop thinking of who you would be

And keep asking the Lord to unveil you

I am along the way to meet you and find the ultimate meaning of life

I am here at my best doing something good

So when I meet you I can give you my all

May you be patient enough to fulfill your dreams

Be bold to explore and learn to know yourself better

So that you will be certain when we meet

Every minute of everyday brings me closer to be with you

and the gentle wind from the North assures me of your existence somewhere reaching out for me.

So, when the chilly winds touches you, know in your heart that we are almost there

I breathe between the line and live in the stain of ink and paper

I am made of words

9 789354 728563

Printed by Libri Plureos GmbH in Hamburg,
Germany